The abilities in me

This book is dedicated to Logan Keir, age 6 with 22q Deletion

Published by The Abilities In Me
Written by Gemma Keir
Illustrations copyright © 2020 by Adam Walker-Parker
Edited by Emma Lusty and Claire Bunyan

ISBN Paperback:9781784566913
ISBN Hardback: 9781784566920
First printed in the United Kingdom, 2019

www.theabilitiesinme.com

The abilities in me

in me

22q deletion

Written by Gemma Keir
Illustrated by Adam Walker-Parker

In a world full of people

I am **different**, that's true.

But what makes me stand out is my 22q.

22q? "What is that?" you may **ask**.

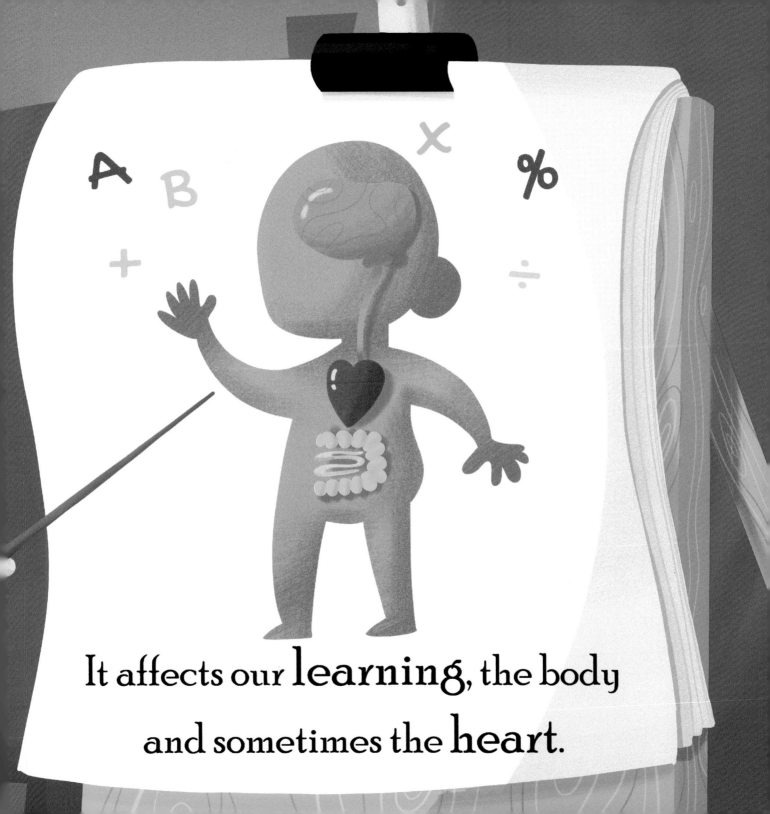

It affects our **learning**, the body
and sometimes the **heart**.

Picture me like a puzzle,

a small piece is not there.

It makes me who I am,

so please, show me you care.

Just like **you**,
I wake up each **day**,
brush my teeth and
get dressed.

Then I have breakfast,
play with my toys
and tidy up the mess.

Sometimes school is **hard** for me.

It can really **affect** my day.

Sometimes I find it **hard** to focus
or **understand** what you say

But school can be really fun!

I like to learn new things.

I love to listen to music

and when we all get to sing.

Sometimes, I need my wheelchair as my legs can feel sore.

Sometimes you may see me excited, running through the hall.

It's nice, when people are **kind** to me and **include** me in their games.

It's nice to make new friends and treat each other the **same**.

When I'm at home with my family,
they give me lots of hugs.

They tell me that they love me
and I love them, very much.

I have my dinner,

get ready for bed,

close my eyes,
it's time to rest.

So now you know about my 22q,

let's be friends

and teach me about you!

Write down your super abilities:

What makes you happy?
Please **draw** below.

What is 22q Deletion?

Also known as DiGeorge Syndrome and Velocardiofacial Syndrome

22q11.2 Deletion syndrome is caused by a small missing piece of chromosome 22. The missing piece of chromosome 22 can affect every system in the human body.

22q can cause up to 180 mild to serious health and developmental issues in children and adults.

It is believed to be the second most common genetic disorder behind Down's Syndrome yet is still relatively unknown to the majority of people. Due to the various symptoms of 22q, it can be difficult for doctors to diagnose. Many children can wait years before a diagnosis is made.

Families of those with 22q are requesting for screening at birth as with early intervention, many lives can be saved. It is believed that around 1 in 4000 estimated number of children are born each year with 22q.

The symptoms most commonly linked to 22q include growth delays, feeding problems, congenital heart disease, gastrointestinal difficulties, serious breathing concerns, cleft and craniofacial issues, calcium deficiencies, immune deficiencies, kidney problems, and skeletal anomalies.

There is also a possibility of developing speech, developmental and cognitive delays, as well as Autism, ADHD, learning disabilities and anxiety.

Find more information at What is 22?
The 22q Family Foundation - Located at 22qfamilyfoundation.org

Max Appeal is a UK registered charity providing information and support to those with 22q11 syndromes.
Our aim is to enable people affected to lead an independent and economically prosperous life as possible with Max Appeal being the voice to achieve appropriate medical care, social support, employment and empowering individuals and their families.

 /MaxAppealUK

Website - www.maxappeal.org.uk

 @MaxAppealUK

The 22q Family Foundation.
Our mission is to raise awareness for 22q11.2 deletion syndrome while connecting, supporting, and providing accurate information to families affected.

Website – www.22qfamilyfoundation.org

 /22qfamily

 @22qfamily

The Foundation is made up of a group that consists of individuals with 22q11.2 Deletion Syndrome, parents, grandparents, siblings and carers of individuals with 22q11.2 deletion Syndrome as well professionals and multidisciplinary staff and researchers.
We support all those affected by 22q through the provision of accurate information, access to education, the fostering of research and the creation of awareness throughout our communities.

/vcfs22q11

Website – www.22q.org.au

@vcfs22q11

Patches Heart Group. We are a support group for children with Congenital heart defects and their families in the community.
We also support many families with children with 22.11q. We offer friendly parent support, information and signposting. Together with our online support group families can access support 24/7.

 /patchesheartgroup   Website - www.patchesheartgroup.org

 @patches22q

About the Author

My name is Gemma Keir, I am the book author for "The abilities in me" children's book series from Hertfordshire, England. I am a mum to a child with a range of medical conditions, including 22q Deletion who has inspired me to write these incredible stories. I am proud to have received qualifications in Special Educational Needs and Disabilities and Sensory Awareness plus specialist training in Behaviour and Safeguarding. These books provide awareness of a range of needs in children today and will be extremely popular for school settings and families who have a child with these conditions. I aim to change the whole perception of these children by promoting the abilities they do have and prevent potential bullying later in that child's life. I feel that this is possible, because children around them will be taught, from a young age and in a positive light, to have awareness and be open-minded. My vision is for children with special educational needs and disabilities to have a book to read about a character who is just like them. I aim to bring inclusivity to children's literature, acceptance and positivity.

www.theabilitiesinme.com

www.facebook.com/theabilitiesinmebookseries

About the Illustrator

My name is Adam Walker-Parker, I am a professional illustrator from Scotland. I have worked in the art industry for 12 years now, I began my career as an artist, choosing to paint figurative and wildlife paintings.
I now illustrate children's books and find joy in creating something magical and inspiring for children to see.

www.awalkerparker.com

www.facebook.com/awalkerparkerillustration

www.instagram.com/awalkerparkerillustration

MORE BOOKS COMING SOON

We create children's picture books, based on characters of young children with varying disabilities. Each book will feature a child with a condition, and we aim to create a bright, colourful and positive outlook on every child with special needs. We are all unique and beautiful in every way, shape and form. This collection of books will show how each child can celebrate their abilities within their disability, find acceptance and create awareness to those around them. These books will touch the hearts of your homes, schools and hospital settings, and most importantly, your child will have a book to read, based on a special character, just like them.

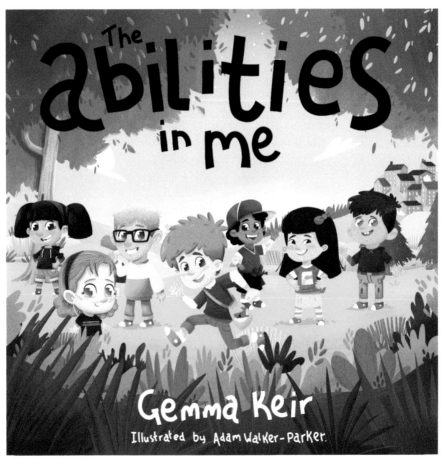

Title: The Abilities In Me - Children's Book Series
Written by Gemma Keir
Cover and Illustrations by Adam Walker-Parker

The abilities in me

BV - #0007 - 010720 - C32 - 216/216/3 [5] - CB - 9781784566920